Original title:
Starting with Me

Copyright © 2024 Swan Charm
All rights reserved.

Author: Paula Raudsepp
ISBN HARDBACK: 978-9916-89-739-3
ISBN PAPERBACK: 978-9916-89-740-9
ISBN EBOOK: 978-9916-89-741-6

My Soul's Clarion Call

In the depths of night, I rise,
A whisper in the silence flies.
Guiding light upon my way,
A beckoning to brighter day.

The stars above bear witness true,
Each twinkle speaks of love anew.
I heed the call; my heart aligns,
In sacred rhythm, my soul shines.

With fervent prayers, I lift my voice,
In faith, my spirit finds its choice.
The path is clear, the journey bold,
In grace and mercy, I am told.

Each gentle breeze, a soft embrace,
Reminds me of the sacred space.
In unity, we stand as one,
Together 'neath the watchful sun.

As echoes of His wisdom ring,
I find the strength in what I bring.
My soul's clarion call, so bright,
Forever led by holy light.

Illuminated Beginnings

In the dawn of every day,
Graceful blessings come my way.
With every breath, a chance to rise,
Illuminated by the skies.

Nature sings a cosmic song,
In unity, where I belong.
The hope of morning, soft and sweet,
A promise where the souls will meet.

In stillness found, I learn to see,
The sacred flow that sets me free.
An open heart, a mind renewed,
In vibrant hues, my spirit glued.

With each encounter, love abounds,
In every heart, the truth resounds.
New beginnings pave the ground,
In faith, our visions are profound.

Illuminated by His grace,
I find my home in every place.
With gratitude, I rise and stand,
Embraced within the Father's hand.

In the Stillness, He Speaks

In the quiet hours of night,
Whispers dance in gentle light.
In the stillness, hearts may hear,
The sacred words that draw us near.

The world might fade to distant sighs,
Yet in this peace, the spirit flies.
Moments cherished, soft and rare,
His presence felt as tender care.

Every thought a prayer ascending,
In silence, all sorrow mending.
With faith ignited, doubts are quelled,
In His embrace, our souls compelled.

Beyond the noise, a truth revealed,
In calmness, all wounds are healed.
The soul finds rest, the heart rejoices,
In silence, we hear the purest voices.

In the stillness, love's refrain,
He speaks to us, and we remain.
Within the quiet, hope ignites,
In sacred whispers, endless nights.

A Covenant with My Heart

With every breath, I make a vow,
To seek His face and humbly bow.
A covenant woven in pure trust,
In faith, I rise from ash and dust.

Each heartbeat echoes love profound,
In sacred space, where grace is found.
He binds my heart with threads of gold,
In every story, prayers unfold.

Through trials faced and mountains climbed,
In every sorrow, joy entwined.
His promises, my guiding star,
In every moment, near or far.

Together, we walk hand in hand,
In unity, I firmly stand.
A covenant treasured, forever sealed,
In His embrace, my soul is healed.

As seasons change and time moves on,
This sacred pact will never be gone.
With gratitude, I whisper sweet,
A covenant with my heart complete.

Anchored in Faith's Embrace

In the stillness, I find peace,
A gentle whisper calls my soul.
With every prayer, my burdens cease,
In His love, I feel whole.

The storm may rage, yet I will stand,
With faith as my guiding light.
In His mercy, my heart is spanned,
Through darkest hours, He's my sight.

Like a lighthouse upon the shore,
He guides my path through trials vast.
With each step, I seek Him more,
In His embrace, fears are cast.

When shadows loom and doubts arise,
I lift my gaze unto the skies.
In every tear, He sees my cries,
His grace, a gift that never dies.

Anchored deep in His great love,
I soar on wings like doves above.
Forever in His arms, I'll stay,
In faith's embrace, I find my way.

The Canvas of My Existence

Each morning paints a brand new dawn,
With colors bright and shadows cast.
The Master's hand, with love is drawn,
In strokes of grace, He holds me fast.

As I walk through fields of strife,
Each step unveils His grand design.
In every challenge, there's new life,
A canvas woven, pure divine.

Through trials faced and battles fought,
His presence lingers close at hand.
In lessons learned, His love is taught,
As I embrace His gentle plans.

The tapestry of joy and pain,
Is laced with threads of hope and fear.
In every joy, in every stain,
His steadfast love is always near.

As the final brushstroke draws near,
I lift my heart in joyful cheer.
For in this life, I'm never lost,
In His art, I'm found at cost.

Worthy of the Sacred Call

With humble heart, I seek the way,
To walk the path that He has laid.
In every word and deed I pray,
To honor Him and not be swayed.

Through trials fierce, my spirit grows,
In every challenge, I find grace.
In faith's embrace, my purpose shows,
To serve, to love, to seek His face.

Worthy am I, though flaws remain,
In His strength, I rise anew.
Each step I take wipes out the stain,
Of past mistakes, I'm bold and true.

With every call, my heart responds,
A servant's heart, I offer free.
In valleys low, to mountains beyond,
His sacred trust has set me free.

In joy and sorrow, I will stand,
Embracing all He's set before.
For in His love, I lend my hand,
To heal and hope forevermore.

The Altar of My Intentions

At dawn I bow my head in grace,
With quiet thoughts that fill this space.
Each wish a candle, softly lit,
In hopes that love and peace will sit.

The silence sings, a gentle prayer,
My heart laid bare, no burdened care.
In faith, I trust the unseen hands,
To guide my steps through life's demands.

I offer dreams upon this stone,
A sacred place where seeds are sown.
With every breath, I feel the flame,
Awakening my spirit's name.

The altar waits for all I share,
Each intention, sweet and rare.
Through trials faced and joys embraced,
In God's embrace, my fears erased.

As twilight falls, I see the light,
Each flicker speaks of hope so bright.
In gratitude, I find my way,
The altar glows, come what may.

Miracles Manifest from Within

In quiet moments, truth reveals,
The power of the heart that heals.
With faith, I plant the seeds of light,
Miracles bloom in darkest night.

Each thought, a spark of divine grace,
Dissolving doubts we often face.
Within my soul, the light does shine,
Connecting all, the blessed vine.

I breathe in hope, exhale the fear,
In silence, find the voice so clear.
The universe conspires to show,
The magic that our spirits know.

With every step, I choose to see,
The beauty of what's meant to be.
In open hands, I offer love,
The blessings pouring from above.

Through faith, the shadows start to fade,
The truth of life, no longer weighed.
Each miracle a gentle gift,
From deep within, my spirit lifts.

A Song of Renewal

In morning light, a new refrain,
Awakening from night's domain.
The song of life begins to play,
   A melody for this new day.

With every breath, I shed the old,
Embracing warmth, the heart is bold.
Renewal flows like rivers wide,
   In joyous dance, my spirit glides.

I sing in praise of every change,
The winding paths that feel so strange.
Suspended moments, rich and rare,
   In gratitude, I lift my prayer.

The echoes of the past resound,
Yet in the present, hope is found.
With open arms, I greet the dawn,
   Each note of life a sacred song.

From ashes rise, the heart reborn,
In every challenge, I am sworn.
A song of renewal starts anew,
With faith, I know I'll see it through.

Tapestry of the Spirit's Journey

In vibrant threads of love and light,
The tapestry unfolds in sight.
Each moment woven with a care,
A story told beyond compare.

With every choice, a stitch we make,
In joy or sorrow, for our sake.
The colors blend, both dark and bright,
An artwork formed in day and night.

Through trials faced and lessons learned,
The spirit's flame within me burned.
Each knot a testament to grace,
In every challenge, I embrace.

As seasons shift, the patterns change,
Our journeys twist, yet feel so strange.
In unity, our hearts entwined,
The fabric of the divine aligned.

Thus, I behold the wondrous whole,
The sacred weave of every soul.
In love's pure light, my spirit soars,
A tapestry that ever pours.

An Offering of Self

In silence I kneel, my heart laid bare,
With open hands, I seek Your care.
Each breath a prayer, a whispered call,
I surrender my all, I give my all.

In shadows cast, Your love will shine,
A guiding light, eternally mine.
With every step, I seek Your grace,
In humble faith, I find my place.

Through trials faced, I'm mold and clay,
Transform my heart, come what may.
With burdens lifted, I rise anew,
In the warmth of love, I find what's true.

In gratitude, I walk this path,
Seeking You in joy, not wrath.
With every choice, my spirit grows,
In each moment, Your presence flows.

Here I stand, an offering pure,
In deep devotion, my heart is sure.
To walk in love, to spread Your truth,
In every stage, reclaim my youth.

Breath of the Believer

In gentle whispers, Your voice I hear,
A sacred breath that calms my fear.
Each moment shared, divinely bright,
In faith I trust, You are my light.

With every dawn, Your love awakes,
A guiding star, my spirit makes.
Among the trials, I find my song,
In breath of faith, I know where I belong.

Through storms that rage, my heart is still,
Your presence there, my deepest will.
In quietude, my soul takes flight,
Embracing truth, surrounded by light.

In every heartbeat, I feel Your grace,
A rhythm thrumming, a sacred space.
As prayers ascend, I'm drawn to You,
In breath of the believer, hope rings true.

With every step, my faith I share,
In joyful trust, I'm held in care.
For in this journey, I am free,
Breath of the believer, alive in Thee.

The Light of New Beginnings

Awake my soul, with morning's glow,
The dawn appears, a promise to sow.
In every moment, possibilities bloom,
The light breaks forth, dispelling gloom.

With open hearts, we greet the day,
In unity, we find our way.
The past behind, the future near,
In the light of hope, we persevere.

Each step taken, a chance to grow,
In shallow waters, or rivers flow.
Leaving behind doubts and fears,
Embracing joy, shedding tears.

In the stillness, Your whispers guide,
In every heartbeat, You reside.
With fresh beginnings, we rise on high,
In gratitude, our spirits fly.

So let us walk, hand in hand,
In the light of love, together we stand.
For every dawn brings a brand new song,
In the light of new beginnings, we belong.

Ascending the Inner Mountain

With faith as a compass, I start to climb,
Each step I take, transcending time.
Through rocky paths, and trails obscure,
In silent strength, my heart is pure.

The mountain rises, steep and tall,
Yet in Your arms, I'll never fall.
With every struggle, I seek the view,
The peak awaits, my spirit's due.

In every breath, I draw You near,
In echoes of faith, I lose my fear.
With every prayer, my spirit soars,
In grace and love, I find the doors.

As the summit beckons, I hear a call,
In the quiet moments, I feel Your thrall.
Each vow renewed, my journey sings,
In ascending faith, the heart takes wings.

And when I reach that sacred space,
I'll find Your light, Your warm embrace.
In the mountain's height, my soul refines,
Ascending the inner mountain, where Your love shines.

Sunlit Roads of Reflection

In the glow of morning light,
We walk the path so bright,
Each step is grace proclaimed,
In silence, we are named.

With each sunbeam gently cast,
We find peace that holds us fast,
Wonders of the heart revealed,
In faith, our wounds are healed.

Shadows softly fade away,
Guided by the light of day,
In every turn, love unfolds,
Stories of the brave and bold.

As we travel hand in hand,
Together, we will stand,
In reflections, souls unite,
Underneath the skies so bright.

In the evening's golden hue,
We find strength to carry through,
With gratitude, our spirits rise,
In the sunset, beauty lies.

Devotion in Daily Life

In the rush of day's embrace,
We seek a sacred place,
Each moment, a prayer spun,
In routine, we have won.

Through simple acts of grace,
We find the holy space,
A smile, a kind embrace,
In love, we find our place.

With every breath, we call,
To lift our hearts, enthrall,
In labor, joy entwined,
A sacred truth defined.

In stillness of the night,
We witness purest light,
Within the quiet soul's sigh,
Devotion never dies.

As dawn breaks once again,
Our spirits rise, unchained,
In the fabric of the day,
Weaving love, come what may.

Fellowship with the Inner Self

In the chamber of the heart,
Where silence plays its part,
We gather thoughts like flowers,
In stillness, find our powers.

With each breath, we delve deep,
Into the soul's mystic keep,
Conversations soft and sweet,
In solitude, we meet.

Voices whisper, softly call,
Guiding truth through every wall,
In reflection, clarity,
Uniting with divinity.

In the temple of our mind,
Wisdom waits, a treasure fined,
Embracing all we hold near,
In love's embrace, no fear.

Through fellowship, we explore,
The sacred self we adore,
In the journey, we shall find,
Unity in heart and mind.

A Heartbeat of Hope

In the pulse of every dream,
Hope flows like a gentle stream,
Carried on the winds of fate,
Whispers of a love so great.

With every dawn's embrace,
We find strength in this grace,
In shadows cast, light appears,
Wiping away our fears.

In the heartbeat of the night,
Stars illuminate our sight,
In the stillness, we take heart,
A sacred journey, a new start.

Embracing all that we face,
In trials, we find our place,
Each tear a drop of faith,
Woven in our endless wraith.

Through the struggles, we shall rise,
With hope lighting up the skies,
In every heartbeat, we shall sing,
A melody of everything.

In the Garden of My Spirit

In the garden of my spirit, I pray,
Nurtured by grace, I kneel each day.
With blossoms of hope and love so pure,
My faith is the soil, steadfast and sure.

Whispers of angels dance in the breeze,
Guiding my heart, bringing me peace.
Each petal a promise, gentle and kind,
In this sacred space, solace I find.

The sun shines bright on the vibrant bloom,
Chasing away shadows that threatened to loom.
In the silence, I hear Your voice,
In my heart's garden, I rejoice.

As I tend to this sacred land,
With every seed, I make my stand.
In trust and surrender, I sow with care,
For I am reminded, You are always there.

So I walk in faith, through joy and despair,
In the lushness of love, I feel You everywhere.
Each moment a miracle, rich and divine,
In the garden of my spirit, my heart will shine.

Rising Monuments of My Faith

In the shadows of doubt, I build my might,
Rising monuments, reaching for light.
With stones of belief and courage so bold,
I craft my story, a legacy told.

Each prayer a brick, each hope a beam,
Framing the path of a vibrant dream.
In faith's stronghold, I will never yield,
With trust in my heart, my spirit's shield.

Through trials faced and battles fought,
Wisdom of ages is dearly sought.
These towers of faith will not crumble nor sway,
For in every heartbeat, You guide my way.

As the sunset paints skies in hues of gold,
I stand resolved, strong and untold.
For in the architect's hand, my vision's clear,
A testament of faith, unshaken by fear.

Rising higher, my monuments gleam,
Reflecting the light of a sacred dream.
In the skyline of promise, my soul takes flight,
To eternal horizons, embracing the night.

The Dawn of Understanding

In the stillness, the dawn begins to rise,
Unfolding mysteries beneath the skies.
With each gentle ray, wisdom draws near,
Illuminating paths, banishing fear.

The whispers of truth in the morning light,
Guide me through darkness, leading me right.
I search for meaning in every small thing,
As the heart learns to dance and to sing.

Embracing the lessons that life has to share,
With open arms, I am willing to dare.
Through questions and trials, I seek to know,
The depth of Your love, the beauty that flows.

In the quiet moments, clarity blooms,
Dispersing the shadows, vanquishing glooms.
With gratitude rising, I lift my voice,
In the dawn of understanding, I rejoice.

Each heartbeat echoes the truths I find,
In the symphony woven, heart and mind.
With each sunrise, anew I begin,
In the dawn of understanding, my soul finds kin.

The Light Within Shines Bright

In the depths of my soul, a flicker ignites,
A flame of divinity, piercing the nights.
With every heartbeat, the light does grow,
Guiding my spirit where love can flow.

In moments of silence, I feel the glow,
A beacon of hope in the ebb and flow.
This sacred light, a gift to embrace,
Illuminates shadows, reveals Your grace.

As the world around me starts to fade,
I find comfort in the love that You've made.
With faith as my anchor, steadfast and true,
The light within shines, only for You.

Through valleys of sorrow and mountains of cheer,
This inner radiance casts away fear.
In the tapestry woven by hands divine,
The light within shines, eternally mine.

With every dawn breaking, a chance to ignite,
The brilliance of spirit that burns ever bright.
I walk in Your wisdom, no longer alone,
For the light within shines, guiding me home.

Mosaics of My Spiritual Journey

In quiet paths, I tread each day,
Where whispers of the heart convey.
The colors blend, a sacred art,
In every piece, God's grace imparts.

The shadows dance beneath the light,
Reflecting faith in endless night.
Each broken shard, a story told,
In every fragment, love unfolds.

With every step, I rise and fall,
Yet in the beauty, I hear the call.
To seek the truth, to spark the flame,
In humble peace, I'll seek His name.

The sacred journey, though it bends,
Brings forth the joy that never ends.
In gratitude, I find my way,
Through every trial, I choose to pray.

A tapestry of grace begins,
Where each lost stitch, the journey spins.
In God's mosaic, I find my peace,
In shattered dreams, my soul's release.

Beauty in the Breath of Being

In morning's light, the dawn unfolds,
A sacred breath, the heart consoles.
In every sigh, divinity sings,
A symphony of life it brings.

The gentle rustle of the leaves,
A song of hope the spirit weaves.
In every heartbeat, love is found,
In quiet moments, grace abounds.

The hummingbird, a fleeting glance,
A testament to life's great dance.
In every creature, every tree,
A whisper of eternity.

With each inhale, I find my place,
In every breath, I'm wrapped in grace.
The essence pure, a gift divine,
In simple joys, our hearts align.

The universe, a canvas wide,
With every breath, we walk beside.
In every moment, beauty's captured,
In sacred stillness, love is raptured.

Homecoming to My True Self

In quiet corners of the soul,
I seek the truth that makes me whole.
The mirror shows my heart's embrace,
In every flaw, I find His grace.

With open arms, I greet the light,
As shadows fade and hope ignites.
The journey back, it leads me near,
To whispered dreams, to love sincere.

In the depths, where waters flow,
I find the seeds of faith I sow.
Through storms that break, I rise anew,
In every tear, His love breaks through.

The path may twist, but still I roam,
In every quest, I find my home.
To stand in truth, to boldly be,
A reflection of divinity.

With every step, my spirit flies,
To realms where only love applies.
In coming back, I find the key,
In knowing Him, I come to me.

The Beatitudes Within

Blessed are the gentle souls,
In meekness, they shall find their goals.
With open hearts, they dare to dream,
In love's embrace, they share the beam.

The mourners hold a sacred space,
In grief, they find the hidden grace.
In tears, the healing starts to flow,
A balm of peace they come to know.

The humble rise in quiet strength,
In every step, they find their length.
The earth shall bear their gentle tread,
A legacy of love is spread.

The merciful grace the world each day,
In kindness, they shall find their way.
For in forgiving, hearts are free,
A testament of unity.

The peacemakers walk in the light,
They turn the dark into the bright.
In every act of love, they win,
The beatitudes abide within.

Awakening the Spirit

In the silence of dawn, hearts align,
Whispers of hope in the gentle sunshine.
With each breath, we rise from the deep,
Awakening spirits that yearn and leap.

A journey begins as the shadows fade,
Guided by faith, no longer afraid.
With hands outstretched to the skies above,
We find the light of divine love.

Beneath the stars, we connect anew,
Filling our souls with a radiant hue.
In the stillness, we hear the call,
United in purpose, we stand tall.

Every step taken, a promise made,
In the garden of grace, we will not be swayed.
With hearts ignited, our spirits soar,
Forever seeking, forever more.

As the sun sets, we gather near,
In unity, we conquer fear.
With prayers lifted, we stand as one,
Awakening spirits, our work begun.

A Journey Within

In the depths of the heart, wisdom calls,
A sacred path where the spirit enthralls.
With courage as guide through shadows we tread,
Finding the light where the lost have fled.

Every question we ask, a door opens wide,
Revealing the truths that within us reside.
When silence surrounds, our minds find their way,
In the journey within, there's much to convey.

With each step we take, the layers peel back,
Shedding the fears that keep us off track.
In the mirror of grace, we see our reflection,
Inhaled by the light, we find our connection.

Through valleys of doubt, and mountains of faith,
The spirit awakens, offering safe wraith.
In the sanctuary of being alone,
We find our purpose, our essence is shown.

So venture within, let the heart lead,
In the garden of truth, plant the sacred seed.
Stand in the stillness, let wisdom unfurl,
A journey within, our gift to the world.

The First Step of Faith

At the edge of the night, a new dawn awaits,
With trembling hearts, we open the gates.
The first step of faith is a whisper so small,
Yet echoes of truth can shatter the wall.

With courage ignited, we venture out wide,
Embracing the unknown, with love as our guide.
Each moment alive, a treasure to hold,
In the stories of faith, the spirit is bold.

As shadows retreat, full of grace we abide,
Finding strength in the journey, eternally tied.
With every heartbeat, our spirits align,
In the tapestry woven, a grand design.

When doubt clouds the mind, and questions ensue,
We stand in the promise, forever anew.
With courage to leap, let your heart take flight,
The first step of faith leads us into the light.

In the chorus of life, we sing our praise,
Embracing the path through the night and the days.
With eyes wide open, our spirits shall soar,
The first step of faith opens every door.

Reflections of the Soul

In the stillness of night, the soul speaks clear,
Mirroring wisdom, banishing fear.
Like ripples on water, we ponder and dwell,
In reflections of grace, our stories we tell.

As we gaze into depths, where shadows reside,
The light of the spirit grants us a guide.
In the dance of existence, we find the embrace,
In reflections of love, we journey with grace.

Through trials and triumphs, the soul learns to sing,
In harmony joined, the eternal springs.
Each moment of struggle, a lesson in gold,
Reflections of the heart, beautiful and bold.

With echoes of prayer floating high on the breeze,
The soul's sacred journey brings us to our knees.
In silence we gather, with hearts intertwined,
Reflections of unity, the ties that bind.

So look to the mirror, let truth be your goal,
In the depths of your spirit, discover your whole.
In reflections of the soul, we rise and unite,
Finding the sacred in all that is light.

The First Step of the Pilgrim

Upon the road, the pilgrim stands,
With faith in heart and open hands.
Each step a whisper, soft and clear,
A call to journey, free from fear.

In twilight's glow, the path unfolds,
The promise of grace, a tale retold.
With every breath, the spirit lifts,
As hope ignites the path of gifts.

Through shadows cast and doubts that wane,
The heart is tethered, free from pain.
Each pebble pressed beneath the toe,
A mark of faith, a sacred flow.

The gathering dusk, the stars ignite,
The pilgrim walks towards the light.
With trust in steps, the soul ascends,
A journey where the spirit mends.

From desolate shores to mountains high,
Each footprint whispered, 'Never die.'
In every turn, a lesson learned,
The flame of faith forever burned.

Rising from the Ashes of Doubt

In silence deep, where shadows creep,
A heart lies broken, hopes asleep.
Yet through the night, a spark remains,
A whispered truth 'midst all the pains.

Like phoenix soaring towards the skies,
From ashes formed, the spirit flies.
With wings of faith, it learns to soar,
A testament to love's great lore.

The fire within ignites the soul,
Each burning question makes it whole.
Emerging strong from trials faced,
The heart reclaims what doubt displaced.

Through darkest nights and endless strife,
The light within renews the life.
Transformation blooms, a sacred dance,
In every heart, there lies a chance.

Embrace the light, let shadows fade,
For in the storm, the truth is laid.
With every tear, a brighter dawn,
From doubt's cocoon, the soul is drawn.

The Sanctuary of Self

In stillness deep, the spirit rests,
A haven found where love invests.
Within the heart, a sacred space,
A tranquil echo, pure embrace.

The whispers soft, like gentle rain,
Wash over wounds, relieve the pain.
In solitude, the truth unfolds,
In every breath, the heart beholds.

Each moment spent, a prayer sincere,
The sanctuary calms the fear.
Embracing flaws, the soul finds grace,
A journey inward to that place.

With open arms, the self is free,
To dance in light, to simply be.
In quietude, the spirit sings,
A melody of simple things.

Each heartbeat echoes love divine,
A refuge built on faith's design.
In every pause, a chance to know,
The sanctuary of self, the flow.

Honoring the Divine Spark

Each soul a spark, a light aglow,
A treasure deep, where love can grow.
In every heart, a fire burns bright,
Reflecting grace in darkest night.

To honor self is to know we're one,
Connected to all, beneath the sun.
In every being, the sacred sings,
A harmony of life that brings.

With every word and every deed,
We plant the seeds of love we need.
To celebrate the spark divine,
Is to embrace the ties that bind.

In service given and kindness shared,
The flame of hope is deeply cared.
With open hearts, we lift the veil,
In unity, we shall prevail.

So let us shine, and let us share,
The light of love that's always there.
In every moment, be aware,
The divine spark is ours to bear.

Discovering Divine Purpose

In the stillness, I seek Your light,
Guiding whispers through the night.
Each step taken, a sacred sign,
In humble trust, I rest in Thine.

Life's vast tapestry unfolds with grace,
Every thread weaves in its place.
Though shadows loom and doubts arise,
I gaze above to find the skies.

Moments of joy, moments of pain,
In suffering, Your love remains.
Through trials faced, I grow so bold,
Unfolding stories yet untold.

With open heart, I walk this road,
Every burden, I cast and unload.
In purpose clear, my spirit thrives,
As I embrace this life that drives.

My soul's journey, a sacred quest,
To see Your image in every rest.
With faith as my shield, I will pursue,
The divine path You laid anew.

My Heart's Prayer for Clarity

Oh Lord, in silence, I come to plea,
For guidance clear, please speak to me.
When doubts arise, and fog surrounds,
Show the way through hallowed grounds.

In choices vast, I seek Your face,
Illuminate with loving grace.
Let every step in faith be sure,
In Your embrace, my heart finds cure.

With every thought, I lay it down,
My restless heart, let peace be found.
In moments of noise, grant me a sign,
A gentle nudge, to know You're mine.

From darkness lift this weary soul,
In Your embrace, I find my whole.
With courage strong, I rise anew,
In clarity, my spirit grew.

In prayer I trust, with heart aligned,
Your purpose, Lord, I seek to find.
As storms may rage and shadows play,
I lean on You, my guiding ray.

Pilgrim on the Path to Wholeness

As a pilgrim, I wander far,
With hope ignited like a star.
Every footprint, a story to tell,
In search of the truth where spirits dwell.

Through valleys deep, and mountains high,
I journey forth, my heart to fly.
In every trial, a lesson learned,
To seek the light for which I've yearned.

In sacred moments, I find my peace,
From worldly weights, my soul's release.
With every breath, I draw You near,
In stillness found, I combat fear.

Compassion blooms along the way,
As I share love, come what may.
In kindness sown beneath the skies,
I see the spark of Your good ties.

On this path, the road may bend,
Yet with each step, You are my friend.
Wholeness calls, and I respond,
In the journey's heart, we are all one.

Harvesting the Fruits of Faith

In fields of blessings, I plant my seed,
With tender care, You meet my need.
In seasons changing, I trust and wait,
For Your promise sown will lead to fate.

Sunshine warms and storms may test,
Yet in Your love, I find my rest.
With gratitude, I gather near,
The fruits of faith, lightens my fear.

Each trial faced a fertile ground,
Where lessons learned are truly found.
From doubt to strength, my heart will sway,
In every harvest, You find a way.

Beneath the weight of life's demands,
Your steady grace upholds my hands.
In unity, we share this plight,
Harvesting hope, a shared delight.

With each new dawn, I lift my song,
In faith, with You, I will belong.
The fruits of love forever bloom,
In every heart, dispelling gloom.

Labyrinth of Personal Revelation

In shadows deep, we seek the light,
Each twist and turn, a prayer ignites.
Through trials faced, we find our way,
In the stillness, Truth will stay.

The heart cries out, a sacred song,
In the maze, together we belong.
With every step, our spirits soar,
To the Divine, we open doors.

In the mirror, we see His grace,
Reflections dance, a holy space.
Lost and found, our souls entwine,
In the labyrinth, His love will shine.

Each choice we make, a guiding star,
In the journey, we wander far.
Yet in His arms, we rest and be,
The labyrinth leads us, we are free.

With humble hearts, we navigate,
To the unseen, we meditate.
In whispers soft, the answers call,
Through revelation, we embrace all.

Echoes of Eloquence in Silence

In the quiet, souls entwine,
A language spoken, pure, divine.
With every breath, a prayer is born,
In silence deep, our hearts are worn.

The stillness speaks, a gentle grace,
In the void, we find our place.
Where words may fail, the spirit thrives,
In hushed tones, the essence drives.

Beneath the noise, a love profound,
In echoes soft, we are unbound.
Listening hearts, we learn to feel,
The sacred truth, the holy real.

In solitude, we seek His face,
Connecting threads of time and space.
For in the silence, we are one,
In unity, our race is run.

Each moment passed, a sacred gift,
In tranquil waves, our spirits lift.
With open hearts, we embrace the light,
In echoes of silence, we unite.

The Language of Grace

In every gesture, in every glance,
The language speaks of love's expanse.
With gentle hands, we weave our fate,
In unity found, we contemplate.

Through trials faced, we learn to grow,
In kindness shared, our spirits flow.
With every breath, a tender sign,
In whispers soft, His heart aligns.

The beauty shines in humble ways,
In every moment, grace conveys.
With open arms, we share the light,
In sacred truths, we seek the right.

In laughter shared and tears released,
The language of grace is never ceased.
In every soul, a story speaks,
A tapestry of love unique.

With hearts ablaze, we rise and soar,
In every challenge, we explore.
With gratitude, we sow the seeds,
In the garden of grace, the spirit feeds.

Self-Discovery through the Divine Lens

In reflection's gaze, we peer within,
A journey starts where we begin.
Through trial and grace, we come to see,
In the mirror, who we're meant to be.

Each step unfolds a sacred path,
In joy and sorrow, we find the math.
Through every problem, we resolve,
In the struggle, our souls evolve.

With open hearts, we seek the truth,
In every heartbeat, the pulse of youth.
The canvas waits for colors bright,
In divine hues, we find our light.

Through sacred texts and whispers soft,
We climb the heights, our spirits loft.
With reverence, we honor the day,
In the lens of the Divine, we sway.

In gratitude, we learn to be,
In self-discovery, we find the key.
The journey calls, and we engage,
Through the Divine lens, we write our page.

Communion with the Inner Self

In stillness found, the spirit knows,
The whispers soft, where truth bestows.
A journey deep, within the soul,
A sacred place, where we are whole.

A quiet heart, a mindful breath,
In silence speak, beyond the death.
With every thought, our essence grows,
And in this peace, our purpose flows.

From swirling doubts, we gently part,
And find the light within the heart.
In sacred union, self embraced,
In every moment, love is graced.

Divine connection, always near,
In moments dark, let light draw near.
Transcending fears, the self awakes,
In pure communion, joy remakes.

We rise as one, in truth's pure glow,
In union found, our spirits flow.
With gratitude, we seek and find,
The path of peace, within the mind.

The Sacred Mirror of the Heart

In every glance, the truth reflects,
A mirror clear, the heart connects.
With love's pure light, we see what's real,
In sacred stillness, wounds can heal.

Through aching trials, we learn to see,
The hidden depths of you and me.
Each tear we shed, a lesson gained,
In each embrace, the soul unchained.

With open hearts, we seek the way,
To understand, to humbly stay.
As shadows dance, in light we trust,
In every moment, love is just.

The sacred mirror holds our dreams,
In its embrace, the spirit beams.
Reflecting grace, the heart's true art,
In every breath, a brand new start.

In silent prayer, we find our place,
The mirror's depth, a warm embrace.
As we behold, we learn to be,
A witness to divinity.

Threads of Faith and Wisdom

In woven strands of life we find,
The tapestry of heart and mind.
Each thread of faith, each whisper true,
In life's great loom, we stitch anew.

Through trials faced and courage shown,
In bonds of love, our essence grown.
With wisdom gained, we find our way,
In darkest nights, we seek the day.

These threads unite, in colors bright,
A sacred dance, a shared delight.
In every knot, a story told,
In every heart, a spark of gold.

With hands entwined, we journey forth,
Embracing all, of humble worth.
As faith unfolds, our spirits soar,
In unity, we seek much more.

We weave together, learn and share,
In threads of kindness, love and care.
Through every trial, wisdom's glow,
Guiding us softly, to the flow.

The Light of Introspection

In quiet moments, wisdom gleams,
The light within, ignites our dreams.
With eyes closed tight, we journey deep,
To sacred places, where secrets keep.

Reflections dance upon the mind,
In shadows cast, we seek to find.
What truth resides, beneath the veil,
In stillness found, our hearts prevail.

Through gentle whispers of the soul,
We sift through thoughts, and find the whole.
In every doubt, the light reveals,
The strength we hold, the love it heals.

In inward gaze, we learn to trust,
The spirit's path, it's gracious thrust.
With every breath, the light shall guide,
In introspection, God's love abides.

With open heart, we face the dawn,
Embracing light, our burdens gone.
Through self-discovery, we ignite,
The sacred flame, in love's pure light.

Cupping the Waters of Blessing

In the stillness of dawn's light,
I gather dew, soft and bright.
Each droplet a whisper divine,
Flowing in grace, your love I entwine.

With open hands, I receive the flow,
Rich blessings that only you know.
Water of life, pure and clear,
A sacred gift that draws me near.

In the depths of my soul, they quench,
Thirst that grows with each faithful wrench.
Cupping the waters, I see the way,
To walk in your light, come what may.

As rivers of mercy, your kindness streams,
Filling my heart, igniting dreams.
With every sip, my spirit will rise,
A song of joy, reaching the skies.

In this chalice of hope, I find my peace,
Every burden you gently release.
With waters of blessing flowing free,
I am one with you, eternally.

The Unfolding of the Heart

Beneath the vast and starry dome,
My heart seeks you, a sacred home.
With each pulse, a prayer takes flight,
In the quiet, your love ignites.

Like petals that open to the sun,
The unfolding begins; we are one.
Layer by layer, I lay it bare,
Trusting your grace, found everywhere.

In your presence, fears break apart,
Illuminating the hidden heart.
Each thought a leaf in the breeze,
Carried by faith, it finds ease.

With every heartbeat, truth is revealed,
Boundless love, our fate sealed.
In vulnerability, I find my might,
The soul's journey, guided by light.

As dawn spreads its wings on the morn,
Awakening visions I've long worn.
The sacred call speaks through the night,
In the unfurling, your grace is my sight.

Intimacy with the Creator

In the silence, a gentle sigh,
Whispers dance as moments fly.
Crafted by hand, the universe spins,
In the depths, our connection begins.

Each breath I take, a love letter penned,
In your embrace, I find my friend.
Threads of fate intertwine our souls,
In the tapestry, your vision unfolds.

With each prayer that rises like smoke,
I feel your essence, so unbroke.
Wrapped in grace, shadows dissolve,
In intimacy, my heart resolves.

Your touch in the breeze, your voice in the rain,
Every heartbeat, a sweet refrain.
In sacred spaces, I find my truth,
A cherished bond, eternal youth.

Together we walk through valleys and peaks,
In silence and joy, it's you that I seek.
In this communion, my spirit is free,
An endless dance, just you and me.

My Spirit's Unwritten Testament

In the shadows of night, I ponder deep,
Words unspoken, secrets I keep.
A testament forged in silence profound,
In the stillness, your wisdom is found.

With ink of faith, on the pages of fate,
I write my truth, no need to wait.
Every struggle, every tear,
Crafts a story that draws you near.

In the laughter, in the pain,
I seek the lessons, the sacred gain.
Through trials that shape my wayward path,
I find your presence in love's warm bath.

Each moment a brushstroke, divine and rare,
Painting my spirit with memories to share.
As time flows gently, I trust your hand,
Guiding this verse to your promised land.

So here it unfolds, as I pen my soul,
In the quiet, you make me whole.
My spirit's testament, a radiant glow,
In your embrace, I conquer all woe.

The Reflection of Devotion

In quiet prayer, the spirit soars,
A whisper soft through opened doors.
With each heartbeat, faith ignites,
Guided by love, our soul unites.

In service pure, we find our way,
Through trials faced, we learn to stay.
A loving hand, in darkness bright,
Devotion blooms, a beacon light.

With gratitude, we bow in grace,
Each moment shared, a sacred place.
In gentle trust, our worries cease,
In Him we find our truest peace.

In silence deep, we hear His call,
A steadfast heart will never fall.
Through joyful hymns and humble tears,
The path unfolds throughout the years.

Eternal light, within us grows,
Through every doubt, His mercy flows.
Together strong, we rise and stand,
In faith's embrace, united hand in hand.

Rooted in Sacred Truth

Beneath the sky, we seek the ground,
In ancient texts, the truth is found.
With every step, we tread with care,
A journey woven in silent prayer.

The sacred whispers through the trees,
In sacred spaces, hearts find ease.
With open minds, we look within,
Reflecting light, where love begins.

As seasons shift and shadows dance,
We find our faith in every chance.
Embracing hope in trials faced,
In sacred truth, our lives are graced.

From humble roots, the spirit thrives,
In every breath, the essence strives.
Together bound, we rise and sing,
In every heart, a sacred spring.

With open arms, we share our song,
In kindness' light, we all belong.
Through unity, our souls will soar,
In love's embrace, we are once more.

A Pilgrimage of the Heart

On winding roads, our spirits climb,
In search of peace, throughout all time.
With every step, our burdens fall,
A pilgrimage to answer the call.

Through valleys deep and mountains high,
We find our strength in faith's reply.
With open hearts, we journey on,
Embracing light, from dusk till dawn.

In sacred silence, we find our way,
A compass guided by love's sway.
With every tear, we cleanse our soul,
In grace's arms, we become whole.

Each sacred moment, a treasure rare,
We walk together, a bond we share.
With hope as our lantern, love as our guide,
In every heartbeat, the Spirit abides.

Through trials faced, we learn to yield,
In faith's embrace, our wounds are healed.
Together we grow, in light and grace,
In every step, we find our place.

Resilience in the Embrace of Spirit

Through storms that rage, our spirits shine,
In trials faced, we trust the divine.
With hearts aflame, we rise anew,
In love's embrace, our faith rings true.

The darkest nights shall pass away,
For dawn shall break, a brand new day.
In every test, our strength endures,
With open hearts, we find the cures.

In whispers soft, His voice will say,
"Fear not, my child, just walk this way."
Through valleys low and hills so steep,
In His embrace, our souls find peace.

Together we stand, unyielding, strong,
With love as our anthem, we'll carry on.
In hands united, we face each fight,
In resilience, we find our light.

With faith as our anchor, we shall thrive,
In struggles faced, our spirits drive.
Through every moment, we learn to trust,
In love's embrace, we rise from dust.

In the Silence of the Soul

In quiet depths, where shadows dwell,
The whispering winds begin to tell.
A stillness wraps the heart so tight,
Creating space for sacred light.

Here in reverie, the spirit stays,
With silent hymns that softly praise.
The echoes dance upon the dawn,
As wisdom blooms, the darkness gone.

In solitude, the soul takes flight,
Embracing grace, embracing night.
Where every breath becomes a prayer,
And peace descends, an answered care.

The universe, a gentle guide,
Transforms the heart, deep joy supplied.
In silence, love reveals its face,
Awakening the soul to grace.

Within the calm, a truth unfolds,
A precious treasure that never grows old.
In silence found, the spirit knows,
A path of light where beauty flows.

Gathering the Fragments of Spirit

Amidst the shards of life's great maze,
We seek the light, we seek the praise.
With every tear, a lesson learned,
In every hope, the heart yearned.

Gather the fragments, let them align,
Infinite love, pure and divine.
In the struggle, find strength anew,
For every broken part holds truth.

The sacred tapestry of grace,
Woven in time, a holy space.
Each thread a story of love unspun,
A journey shared, we are all one.

In humble hearts, the pieces mend,
Through faith and love, we transcend.
The spirit soars, the shadows flee,
In gathered fragments, we are free.

Together we rise, in unity sing,
Each note a blessing, each breath a wing.
In gathering strength, the soul ignites,
In the dance of life, the spirit delights.

The Echoes of Divine Love

In the stillness, love's voice resounds,
A melody of grace that astounds.
From heights unseen, it stirs the heart,
Binding the universe, never apart.

With every heartbeat, the echoes rise,
Reflections of love that never dies.
Through trials faced and mountains moved,
In every moment, we are soothed.

Like gentle rains, love falls anew,
Quenching the thirst of our yearning view.
In the embrace of time and space,
Divine love flows, a warm embrace.

From realms above, the whispers call,
Through laughter shared and shadows fall.
In every gesture, a light persists,
Love's echo lives in the soul's tryst.

When doubt creeps close, hear love's refrain,
In every loss, and in every gain.
The echoes linger, forever clear,
Our hearts awaken when love is near.

Harvesting the Fruits of Reflection

In quiet moments, the mind will roam,
To seek the truth, to find our home.
Through seasons past, the lessons grow,
Harvesting wisdom from seeds we sow.

The fruits of thought, ripe and sweet,
Offer nourishment in life's retreat.
With every pause, a sacred chance,
To glean the gifts from life's expanse.

Amidst the trials, in shadows cast,
Lies golden insight from the past.
In reflections deep, the spirit sings,
Revealing treasures that true love brings.

With every sigh, we gather grace,
In every tear, a sacred space.
The heartache fades, the joy will rise,
In harvesting love, we realize.

So let us dwell where beauty grows,
In every season, our spirit flows.
For in reflection, the soul expands,
Harvesting fruits from divine hands.

Surrendering to the Divine Within

In silence, I find my grace,
A whisper deep within my soul.
I bow my head, I seek Your face,
In tender peace, I feel made whole.

With every breath, I let You in,
My heart a vessel pure and bright.
I surrender all my sin,
To guide me through the darkest night.

Your love, a flame that burns so clear,
In chaos, You bring calm and light.
I follow where You steer me near,
Divine embrace, my spirit's flight.

In trust, I place my fragile heart,
Each moment, gifts of love I see.
No longer do we stand apart,
With You, forever, I am free.

The Hymn of New Beginnings

Awake, O heart, to morning's song,
In fields of grace, let hope arise.
Each dawn shines bright, where I belong,
With faith that opens up the skies.

The past is but a whispered breeze,
In every leaf, a tale retold.
I seek the path where I find ease,
With You, my journey's dreams unfold.

In tender blooms of joy, I stand,
The earth awakens from its sleep.
With open arms, I heed Your hand,
In faith, the promises I keep.

O Spirit, guide my every step,
Through trials fierce and skies so gray.
In love, I wake, in light, I prep,
A hymn of hope to light my way.

Awakening the Sacred Within

Beneath the stars, I close my eyes,
A sacred voice begins to rise.
In stillness found, my heart obeys,
The whispers of the ancient ways.

The rhythm of the earth I hear,
In nature's song, Your truth appears.
Awakening this sacred spark,
Illuminates the quiet dark.

With each heartbeat, I ignite,
The love that breathes in purest light.
In every prayer, my spirit soars,
Throughout the world, my heart explores.

In sacred circles, grace flows free,
United in our unity.
Awakening the truth within,
The journey starts where love begins.

Journey to the Divine Heart

In search of peace, I roam the land,
With every step, Your light I seek.
With faith, I rise, I make my stand,
I follow You, my heart's true peak.

Through mountains high and valleys wide,
Your presence guides, I feel the flow.
With each dawn's light, my fears subside,
In shadows deep, Your love I know.

The river's song, so pure and clear,
Reminds me of Your endless grace.
With open heart, I draw You near,
In every moment, I embrace.

Through trials faced and joys anew,
I walk the path, Your will be done.
In every heartbeat, love shines through,
A journey blessed, my spirit's run.

The Song of the Soul's Awakening

In silence deep, the spirit stirs,
A whisper soft, in sacred purrs.
From shadows cast, the light breaks through,
Awakening dreams, both pure and true.

With every breath, the heart will sing,
To fields of grace, our souls take wing.
In unity, we rise and soar,
A chorus rich, forevermore.

The dusk gives way to morning's breath,
As life unfolds, defying death.
In sacred dance, we find our place,
The song of love, the saving grace.

Awakening deep, beneath the skin,
We step into the world, within.
Carried forth on winds of light,
In every dawn, our spirits bright.

With open hearts, we seek the way,
In pursuit of truth, we humbly pray.
In the garden of faith, we find our voice,
In the joy of light, our souls rejoice.

Illuminating the Inner Darkness

In caverns deep, where shadows lie,
A flicker bright, a spark to try.
Through veils of doubt, we search for light,
In every dark, there blooms the bright.

With courage sought, we face the fear,
In trembling hearts, the truth draws near.
A beacon shines through tempest's night,
Illuminating souls with light.

In sacred trust, we walk the path,
And turn away from whispered wrath.
With each step forward, shadows flee,
In inner light, we come to be.

Awake, arise, the world unfolds,
In warmth embraced, our story told.
Through hidden trials, grace will steer,
In darkened realms, the light is near.

The journey long, but worth the fight,
We find our way, through endless night.
With faith unshaken, hearts refined,
In love's embrace, we're intertwined.

Anointing the Heart's Desire

In stillness found, the heart does yearn,
A sacred fire, for love we burn.
With open hands, we seek the balm,
Anointing dreams, our spirits calm.

With gentle grace, our paths unfold,
In whispered prayers, our hopes retold.
In gratitude, we weave our fate,
For every wish, the love innate.

Through trials faced, our souls ignited,
In darkness met, the heart united.
The essence pure, flows like a stream,
In every heartbeat, there lies a dream.

Anointing tears, the soul's release,
With every ache, we find our peace.
In faith, we trust, the journey's way,
To follow light, we safely stray.

In sacred moments, love abounds,
The heart's desire, where grace surrounds.
With humble joy, our spirits rise,
In every dawn, our hearts shall prize.

The Dawn of Personal Reverence

At morning's light, a promise heard,
In hushed tones, a whispered word.
With reverence, we honor each breath,
In gratitude, we dance with death.

In sacred stillness, we find our place,
Within the heart, a loving space.
Where every soul is free to roam,
In unity, we find our home.

With gentle hands, we lift the veil,
To see the truth, and not to pale.
In every glance, a spark ignites,
As reverence dawns, the spirit lights.

Through trials faced, we learn to bend,
In loving kindness, wounds we mend.
With every sunrise, wisdom grows,
In every heart, the love still flows.

In humble awe, our spirits soar,
As dawn breaks forth, we seek for more.
With reverent hearts, we journey forth,
To greet each day, a precious birth.

A Testament of Self

In the stillness, I seek the light,
A journey within, ignited by grace.
Each breath a prayer, each thought a fight,
To unravel the truth in my sacred space.

The echoes of doubt, they linger still,
Yet hope arises from shadows past.
In the whispers of faith, I find my will,
A testament of self, anchored and steadfast.

With every falter, I rise anew,
Each stumble a step toward the Divine.
In love and in wisdom, my heart breaks through,
Awakening purpose in every line.

The mirror reflects the soul's embrace,
A tapestry woven with threads of light.
In silence, I find my sacred place,
Where I stand renewed, ready for flight.

In the garden of being, I plant my seed,
Nurtured by kindness, watered by tears.
With courage and patience, I fulfill my need,
To bloom in the presence of my deepest fears.

The Whisper of the Heart

In the quiet dawn, a soft voice stirs,
Guiding the soul through the morning mist.
Gentle and pure, the truth occurs,
A whisper of love in the light's gentle twist.

The heart knows secrets that time may hide,
A melody sweet that resonates deep.
In every heartbeat, in every tide,
Lies the wisdom of promises we keep.

To listen closely, to heed the call,
In moments of silence, we find our way.
The whispers of mercy, though silent to all,
Speak volumes of grace in the break of day.

In surrender, we find a strength rare,
The courage to walk on paths unknown.
Each whisper a beacon, a soft loving care,
Guiding us back to the love we've outgrown.

As twilight descends, the whispers remain,
In shadows and dreams, let them guide you home.
For in every heart, through joy and through pain,
The whisper of the heart teaches us to roam.

Pilgrimage to the Divine

Beneath the vast and starlit sky,
I take my steps with faith as my guide.
Each footprint echoes a silent cry,
A pilgrimage to the Divine inside.

Through valleys low and mountains high,
I wander where the spirit calls.
With every challenge, I spread my wings,
In search of grace through life's great thralls.

In nature's temple, I kneel and pray,
The whispering winds carry my dreams.
In shadows and light, I find my way,
Awakening truth in life's flowing streams.

The journey is long, yet I shall not tire,
For every moment is sacred and bright.
In love, I walk, igniting my fire,
A pilgrimage leading me back to the light.

In unity sought, I find my place,
Together with souls that seek and ascend.
In the heart's embrace, I find my space,
A pilgrimage to the Divine, a journey without end.

The Altar of Introspection

Before the altar, I lay my soul,
Each thought a letter, each sigh a prayer.
In stillness, I seek to become whole,
A sacred moment, a truth laid bare.

The echoes of past in gentle refrain,
Guide me through shadows of doubt and fear.
Here, in the silence, I witness the pain,
Embracing the lessons that brought me here.

With candlelight flickering, I sit and see,
The choices I've made, each joy, each fall.
In reflection's embrace, I set my spirit free,
Transforming the darkness into the call.

At the altar of introspection, I stand,
Awakening strength that's buried deep.
With grace as my armor and love in hand,
I celebrate the journey, the sowing I reap.

In the stillness found, I hear my truth,
A melody rising from depths within.
At the altar of life, I reclaim my youth,
In every heartbeat, I start again.

Reflections of Faith Unveiled

In silence, my heart seeks the divine,
Each prayer a whisper, a sacred sign.
Hope weaves through shadows, bold and bright,
Guiding my soul toward the light.

With every struggle, I learn to stand,
Trusting the grace of a guiding hand.
In doubt's embrace, I find my way,
Faith, a beacon, come what may.

The trials faced, a pathway paved,
In valleys low, my spirit's saved.
Each tear I shed, a lesson learned,
In love's pure fire, my heart is burned.

In moments of fear, I still find peace,
The promise of hope that will never cease.
A journey long, yet I am whole,
In faith's embrace, I find my soul.

At twilight's hour, I kneel and pray,
Thankful for light that guides my way.
With open arms, the Spirit calls,
In faith, my heart forever falls.

Seeds of Grace Planted

With humble hearts, we sow our seeds,
In fields of love, where faith exceeds.
Tending to souls with gentle care,
Each moment cherished, each whispered prayer.

In every kindness, grace is found,
Roots intertwined in sacred ground.
Through storms of life, we stand as one,
Harvest of joy beneath the sun.

From burdens shared, the Spirit grows,
A garden rich, where mercy flows.
In hearts awakened, dreams take flight,
Together we rise, bathed in light.

With tending hands, we nurture peace,
In love's embrace, our worries cease.
A tapestry woven, strong and true,
In every thread, the grace shines through.

As seasons change, our spirits gleam,
Trust in the path, and nurture the dream.
For every heart that joins in praise,
Together we dance in grace's gaze.

The Path to Inner Light

In stillness, the soul begins to see,
The truth that whispers, sets it free.
With every step down heaven's way,
Inner light guides the night to day.

Through trials faced, we find our voice,
In searching hearts, we make the choice.
To walk the path with love embraced,
Toward the light, our fears erased.

Each moment cherished, a chance to grow,
As wisdom deepens in ebb and flow.
Through valleys dark, we seek the flame,
A light within, forever the same.

In grace we rise, our spirits soar,
Trusting the path, we ask for more.
In sacred silence, we find our peace,
The journey blooms, our souls release.

With every dawn, a promise made,
To seek the light, no fears dismayed.
Together, hand in hand we fight,
Onwards we go toward inner light.

Embracing the Spirit's Whisper

In quiet moments, the Spirit speaks,
A gentle voice the weary seeks.
In shadows cast, we feel the grace,
Embracing love in every place.

Through trials faced, we learn to see,
That faith's true power sets hearts free.
With open arms, we greet the day,
As whispers guide us on our way.

In every challenge, strength takes flight,
Illuminated by sacred light.
The Spirit dances in joy's embrace,
In every tear, we find our place.

Awake, O heart, to life anew,
With every thought, let kindness brew.
In stillness found, we hear the call,
In Spirit's arms, we rise, we fall.

Each whispered prayer, a thread divine,
Weaving hearts and souls in line.
Together we stand, hand in hand,
Embracing love, a sacred band.

Embracing the Inner Light

In the silence, whispers glow,
A gentle spark, a truth to show.
Within the heart, a flame ignites,
Guiding souls through darkened nights.

Hands uplifted, prayers take flight,
In humble focus, we find our might.
Each breath a gift, each moment pure,
In love's embrace, our spirits endure.

Chasing shadows, doubts may arise,
Yet in our depths, the answer lies.
Awakening joy, surrendering fear,
To the inner light, we draw near.

Unity blossoms, spirits entwined,
In sacred space, true peace we find.
Radiant visions, beyond the veil,
Together we journey, we shall prevail.

Embracing the light, we rise as one,
Under the stars, guided by the sun.
In every heartbeat, divinity sings,
We, the children of sacred things.

The Call to the Sacred

A whisper dances through the trees,
Echoing gently on the breeze.
A call that stirs the soul awake,
To seek the paths that love can make.

In every moment, truth is found,
In humble hearts, where hope is sound.
The sacred call, a vibrant song,
Inviting us to join the throng.

With open hands, we gather near,
In shared devotion, we conquer fear.
The sacred flame, it flickers bright,
Illuminating the paths of light.

We travel onward, side by side,
Bound by faith, our hearts as guide.
Through valleys deep and mountains high,
The call to the sacred draws us nigh.

Each step we take, a dance of grace,
In unity, we find our place.
A symphony of spirits strong,
Together we rise, where we belong.

Rooted in Belief

In grounded truth, we find our core,
Roots that anchor, hearts that soar.
Through trials faced and joys embraced,
In faith's embrace, we're interlaced.

With sacred trust, we walk the line,
A journey blessed, our souls align.
In storms we stand, in calm we grow,
The spirit's strength begins to show.

From ancient whispers, wisdom flows,
In the stillness, our knowing grows.
Each doubt released, each fear quelled,
In the light of truth, we are upheld.

Together we rise on wings of prayer,
Rooted in belief, we journey where
Love conquers all, and unity reigns,
In the heart's garden, nothing wanes.

A sacred bond, our spirits entwine,
In the roots of faith, forever we shine.
With every heartbeat, a rhythm divine,
Rooted in belief, our souls align.

The Seed of Divinity

In the silence, a seed is sown,
A spark of light, eternally grown.
Within the soul, a whisper calls,
The seed of divinity, it enthralls.

Nurtured by love, nourished by grace,
In every heart, it finds its place.
From dreams that flutter, to hopes that soar,
The seed of divinity yearns for more.

With every breath, we cultivate,
In unity, we elevate.
In sacred gardens, the spirit blooms,
Filling the air with fragrant plumes.

Through trials and joys, it finds its way,
In the depth of night, it seeks the day.
Boundless potential, alive with zest,
The seed of divinity, forever blessed.

In every soul, a journey starts,
The sacred seed within our hearts.
Together we gather, together we rise,
The seed of divinity opens our eyes.

In Search of Holy Grace

In shadows deep, where silence dwells,
I seek the light, where mercy swells.
With humble heart, I raise my plea,
Grant me the grace to truly see.

Through trials faced, my spirit bends,
Yet whispers of hope, my soul defends.
In every tear, a prayer taking flight,
Leading me onward, toward the light.

Oh, guide my steps on sacred ground,
Where peace and love together abound.
In faith I walk, unburdened, free,
Embracing the joy of what can be.

With every breath, I seek Your face,
In every moment, Your warm embrace.
As dawn unfolds, new mercies flow,
In search of grace, my heart will grow.

So here I stand, in quiet prayer,
Awake, aware, and free from care.
In service, love, my spirit's plea,
In search of grace, I'm one with Thee.

The Path of Inner Sanctity

Upon this path of sacred stone,
I walk alone yet not unknown.
Each step I take, a deeper quest,
To find the peace, to know the rest.

In moments still, Your voice I hear,
A soothing whisper, calm and near.
As shadows fade, I see the way,
Where light and love forever stay.

The trials faced, the burdens borne,
In each experience, I am reborn.
Though storms may come, my spirit stays,
Upon the path of holy ways.

With open heart, I seek to share,
The love divine, the endless care.
In every soul, the spark I see,
The path of sanctity sets us free.

So through the dusk, into the dawn,
With faith unshaken, I press on.
In Your embrace, my journey's creed,
The path of grace, my soul's true need.

Unveiling the Inner Temple

Within my heart, a temple lies,
A sacred space, where spirit flies.
With every breath, I seek the door,
To find the truth, to be restored.

In quietude, the veil does lift,
Revealing love, a precious gift.
In stillness found, the echoes call,
Awakening the heart of all.

With gentle hands, I clear away,
The doubts and fears that lead astray.
To worship now, in purest form,
Embracing grace within the storm.

In joy, I dance, in peace I dwell,
Unveiling light, I heed the bell.
A symphony of hope and grace,
In this inner temple, my sacred place.

So here I stand, with heart laid bare,
In this sanctuary, the soul laid there.
Each moment cherished, each breath a hymn,
Unveiling love that will not dim.

The Prayer of the Unseen

In whispers soft, a prayer does weave,
Through realms unseen, we dare believe.
With hearts aligned, we seek the light,
A sacred bond, ignited bright.

In darkness deep, the spirit glows,
Awakening life, as love bestows.
In quiet moments, truth we find,
The unseen hand that touches mind.

A prayer ascends, unbroken chain,
Connecting souls through joy and pain.
With every sigh, our hopes take flight,
In woven threads of pure delight.

So let us stand, with faith embraced,
In the unseen, our fears erased.
Together we rise, in harmony's song,
The prayer of the unseen, where we belong.

In unity, we boldly seek,
With tender hearts and voices meek.
Through layers thick, we reach the Divine,
In the prayer of the unseen, love intertwines.

Chronicles of Sacred Awakening

In the silence of the dawn's embrace,
I seek the whisper of Your grace.
Each breath a prayer, each heart a song,
In sacred stillness, where I belong.

Waves of wisdom crash on shores,
Unfolding truth as my spirit soars.
In the garden of faith, seeds take root,
With every moment, a holy pursuit.

Light breaks through the shadows' veil,
Guiding me on this divine trail.
With trust, I open my weary heart,
In Your love, I find my part.

Each step a testament, engraved in time,
In the rhythm of prayer, I learn to climb.
With arms lifted high, I surrender my will,
In the embrace of the sacred, I find peace still.

In the dance of being, I find my way,
With every heartbeat, I choose to stay.
Chronicles written in sacred ink,
In this journey of spirit, I seek to drink.

The Offering of My Being

I stand before You, humbled and bare,
My heart a vessel, my soul laid bare.
In the stillness, I bring my plea,
An offering of my entire being, free.

With every breath, I surrender control,
Aligning my spirit, nourishing my soul.
In the light of Your presence, I find my way,
With gratitude blooming, come what may.

Each moment a chance to grow and transcend,
A prayerful whisper, a call to mend.
I offer my trials, my joy, my strife,
In the tapestry woven, the fabric of life.

Through shadows and light, I walk with intent,
My path illuminated, my spirit content.
The offering of love, a sacred bond,
In the embrace of Your grace, I respond.

In each act of kindness, a glimpse of You,
As I seek to live life, holy and true.
My being, my all, cradled in light,
In this sacred journey, I take flight.

Finding God in the Depths of Me

In the caverns of silence, I delve deep,
Where echoes of prayer softly weep.
In the darkest corners, where shadows reside,
I find You waiting, my sacred guide.

With every tear, a truth unveiled,
In the stillness, my spirit prevailed.
In the depths of sorrow, I see Your face,
In the heartache, there lies Your grace.

I journey inward, seeking the light,
Through the valleys of doubt, into the night.
In the labyrinth of fears, I uncover the key,
A pathway leading straight to Thee.

With faith as a compass and love as my song,
I dance through the darkness, where I belong.
Each heartbeat a hymn, each thought a prayer,
In the depths of my being, You are there.

In the whispers of hope, in the breath of peace,
I find my strength and my sweet release.
Through the layers of life, I come to see,
The sacred existence of God in me.

Vessel of My Beliefs

In the hollow of my heart, beliefs reside,
A vessel of faith, my spirit my guide.
With every choice, a sacred decree,
In the ocean of love, I learn to be free.

Layered in wisdom, my soul does bloom,
In the warmth of Your light, dispelling all gloom.
Through trials and triumphs, I carry the flame,
In this sacred journey, I heed Your name.

With open hands, I share my truth,
In the dance of compassion, igniting my youth.
In the tapestry woven, each thread a prayer,
A testament to faith, beyond compare.

In the echoes of kindness, I find my way,
As the tides of belief guide each new day.
My vessel, my heart, filled with grace,
In the river of hope, I find my place.

As light beams within, I'm anchored and whole,
Each moment of love, nurturing my soul.
In the vessel of beliefs, I rise and sing,
In the embrace of Your promise, my heart takes wing.

Heart of a Believer: A Personal Odyssey

In whispers soft, the Spirit calls,
Guiding the heart through shadowed halls.
With faith as light, I tread the way,
Finding grace in each new day.

The path is winding, steep and long,
But every trial makes me strong.
In valleys deep and mountains high,
I lift my gaze and trust the sky.

Each step I take, a prayer I weave,
In every breath, my soul believes.
For in His presence, hope abounds,
And every silence sings profound.

With courage firm, I press on still,
Embracing love, surrendering will.
In unity, the journey shared,
A tapestry of souls laid bare.

Through storms that test, my spirit grows,
In faith's embrace, the truth bestows.
For in the heart of every trial,
Lies the strength to walk each mile.

The Flame of Hope Ignited

In the night, when shadows creep,
A flickering flame stirs from sleep.
It dances bright, defying dark,
A beacon lit, a holy spark.

With every breath, the fire sighs,
Igniting dreams, lifting our eyes.
It whispers warmth to every heart,
Promising peace, a fresh new start.

Though winds may howl and doubts may rise,
The flame of hope will never die.
In trials faced, it fiercely glows,
A steadfast light that gently shows.

From ashes deep, new life begins,
A sacred strength through all our sins.
With faith ignited, love prevails,
Together we will brave the gales.

So cherish well this Holy Fire,
It fuels our dreams, our great desire.
In unity, we carry forth,
The Flame of Hope, our truest north.

Threads of Faith Woven Tight

Each thread a story, woven fine,
In patterns bright, His love divine.
With every knot, a prayer is spun,
A tapestry of hearts as one.

Through joys and sorrows, we entwine,
In every tear, the grace we find.
Together strong, we cannot break,
These threads of faith that we partake.

In colors rich, the fabric glows,
A sacred bond that always grows.
Through trials faced and laughs we share,
We find our strength in faith and prayer.

So let us weave with tender hands,
A life of love, as He commands.
For in this quilt of hope and light,
We cover all, in warmth unite.

With gratitude, we raise our song,
For in His arms, we all belong.
These threads of faith, forever tight,
Guide us on through darkest night.

Journeying to the Source of Serenity

In quiet woods where whispers dwell,
I seek the peace where spirits swell.
With every footfall on this ground,
A sacred space, my heart is found.

The stream flows soft, its waters clear,
In its embrace, I shed my fear.
Each ripple sings of grace untold,
A melody of love unfolds.

The mountains stand, a sentry strong,
Their silent watch, a guiding song.
Through every trial, I find my way,
In nature's arms, I cease to stray.

The breeze, a caress, whispers low,
In stillness sought, my spirit grows.
For in this journey toward the light,
I find my soul, wrapped warm and tight.

So let me wander, free and bold,
Toward every truth that must be told.
For in the source of serenity,
I glimpse the divine, eternity.

The Awakening of the Inner Sage

In silence deep, the soul does stir,
A whisper calls, in dreams confer.
The light within begins to glow,
Guiding paths we long to know.

Through shadowed woods, we seek the truth,
With faith like fire, we spark our youth.
The sage within, a treasure found,
In every heart, where love is crowned.

Each thought a seed, in fertile ground,
With gentle hands, our purpose bound.
The mind a mirror, reflecting vast,
With wisdom deep, we break the cast.

Let doubts dissolve, like mist at dawn,
Embrace the light, let fear be gone.
The inner sage, so wise, so pure,
In every soul, a love mature.

Awaken now, to truths so grand,
In unity, we take our stand.
For in this life, we seek to know,
The inner sage, our hearts aglow.

Offering Up the Heart

With open palms, we lift our plea,
To realms above, where spirits flee.
An offering of love so bright,
Entwined in faith, a sacred light.

In every breath, a prayer takes flight,
In darkest hours, we seek the right.
Each heartbeat echoes, truth be heard,
In silence soft, our souls are stirred.

The burdens laid upon the ground,
In giving, grace and peace abound.
With every tear, we cleanse the soul,
In vulnerability, we feel whole.

Let kindness flow like rivers wide,
In sharing joy, we turn the tide.
An offering, not just a part,
We gift our hopes, we offer heart.

As morning breaks, the shadows flee,
With open hearts, we search the sea.
In love, we find our truest part,
In unity, we offer heart.

The Covenant of Self-Realization

Within the heart, a promise swells,
In whispered vows, the spirit dwells.
A covenant made with the divine,
To seek the truth, our souls entwine.

In every choice, a path unfolds,
Revealing treasures, never told.
With courage fierce, we take the leap,
In trust we sow, in hope we reap.

The mirror reflects our hidden fears,
In facing shadows, we dry our tears.
Each moment lived, a chance to grow,
In the light of love, our essence glow.

Embrace the journey, let it be free,
For in our hearts, we find the key.
A covenant forged in sacred space,
In self-realization, we find grace.

With every step, the path we tread,
In unity with all, we're led.
The covenant strong, through every call,
In self-realization, we rise, we fall.

The First Light of Revelation

In the stillness of the night,
A spark ignites, revealing light.
The dawn awakens, truths unfold,
In gentle whispers, stories told.

With every ray, new insights bloom,
In shadows cast, we find the room.
The heart is opened, wide and free,
In divine guidance, we see the sea.

The first breath drawn, a life anew,
In every heartbeat, love shines through.
The layers peel, the soul laid bare,
In the light of truth, we find our care.

With open eyes, we witness grace,
Each revelation, an embrace.
The journey starts, with faith as crest,
In the first light, we find our rest.

So let us rise, with hope in hand,
In unity, together we stand.
For in this light, we find our way,
The first light of revelation leads the day.

Revelations at Dawn's Door

At dawn's door, the light spills free,
Voices of hope rise, calling me.
In shadows deep, I find the grace,
A moment divine, time shall not erase.

The sun awakes, the world anew,
With every beam, my spirit grew.
Whispers of wisdom dance in the air,
Hearts unite in fervent prayer.

Nature sings of ages past,
In sacred whispers, the truths amassed.
Through trials faced, we stand as one,
Guided by love till the day is done.

The breeze carries prayers, soft and bright,
A promise of peace in the morning light.
Each breath a pledge to walk your way,
In every dawn, I see the day.

So here I stand, with faith in hand,
In the quiet hour, I understand.
Revelations bloom with the rising sun,
A journey begun, let your will be done.

A New Dawn of Belief

When the sky blushes in gold,
Hope is reborn, stories unfold.
A heart once weary, now flies high,
With every sunrise, the spirit sighs.

In the dawn's light, I seek the way,
Trusting the promise of each new day.
Guided by stars that seldom wane,
Through valleys of doubt, I'll break the chain.

With every heartbeat, I feel the call,
A echo of faith that never falls.
As shadows retreat, I glimpse the truth,
In the embrace of love, there lies my proof.

Each moment cherished, each whisper clear,
In the warmth of dawn, I cast off fear.
For in the light, belief will thrive,
A renewed spirit, in grace alive.

So hand in hand, let us arise,
Under the vast and open skies.
A new dawn beckons, bright and bold,
In its embrace, our stories told.

Chosen for the Journey Ahead

I stand before the open road,
Chosen for the paths foretold.
With heart aglow, I take the first step,
In faith I forge, in hope I prep.

A journey long, with trials steep,
In quiet moments, my soul shall keep.
For every challenge, a lesson learned,
In every storm, my spirit burned.

With open arms, I seek the light,
In darkened valleys, I'll find the bright.
For each step forward, a bond is made,
In grace I walk, in love I'm stayed.

The wind whispers tales, ancient and true,
Of souls before, guiding me through.
With every heartbeat, the promise grows,
In trusting faith, my spirit knows.

Chosen and blessed, I journey on,
In search of purpose, till the dawn.
With courage my guide, I'll face the tides,
In this sacred quest, my heart abides.

Whispered Prayers of Resolve

In the silence, hearts draw near,
Whispered prayers, both sweet and clear.
With every sigh, a hope ascends,
In faithful trust, the spirit bends.

The echoes of love dance in the air,
In troubled times, we find our share.
Each solemn wish, a gentle plea,
In unity, we're bound to see.

With steadfast hearts, we rise above,
In trials faced, we learn to love.
Each moment cherished, a sacred vow,
In whispered prayers, we find our now.

A light ignites in darkness cast,
Through whispered prayers, shadows pass.
In the stillness, resolve is found,
A sacred bond that knows no bound.

So gather close, let voices sway,
With whispered prayers, we find our way.
In every heart, a flame we hold,
Guided by faith, our stories unfold.

Sacred Echoes of My Existence

In silence deep, I hear the call,
The whispers of love, that cradle us all.
Each moment a gift, a transient grace,
In the heart's quiet chamber, I find my place.

From ashes we rise, from dust we begin,
Awakening paths where the light can win.
With open arms, I welcome the dawn,
As shadows disperse, my spirit is drawn.

In every heartbeat, a song is sung,
In sacred rhythms, my soul's been sprung.
I walk this journey with faith as my guide,
With love as my armor, there's nothing to hide.

The stars above twinkle like dreams,
Divine reflections in cosmic streams.
I find my solace in nature's embrace,
Each breath a reminder of boundless grace.

Eternal connections bind us as one,
Each path we traverse, the web has begun.
In the sacred echoes, I hear the truth,
A timeless assurance, the spirit of youth.

Divine Inspiration from Within

In quietude, I seek your light,
A spark of wisdom, shining bright.
From depths of being, a vision grows,
In every heartbeat, Your love bestows.

Awakening dreams, like morning rays,
In silent prayer, my spirit sways.
Your voice is the wind, soft in my ear,
Encouraging courage, dissolving fear.

In every moment, your presence flows,
Through trials faced, the heart still knows.
The tapestry woven with threads of grace,
United in purpose, we find our place.

When doubt clouds the path, I shall see,
Your light illuminating the way for me.
In the sanctuary of my tranquil mind,
The answers emerge, in stillness defined.

Oh, divine spirit, in me reside,
Your wisdom my compass, my faithful guide.
In every breath, I am reborn,
With newfound strength, each day is adorned.

The Well of Inner Wisdom

Within the heart lies a sacred well,
Where whispers of truth and knowing dwell.
I draw from depths, each lesson clear,
In reflection's mirror, I find you near.

Through waters calm, the soul does seek,
The strength to rise when I am weak.
Each drop a promise of love's embrace,
In the gentle flow of infinite grace.

With every ripple, wisdom expands,
Guiding my footsteps, molding my hands.
The anchor of faith in turbulent seas,
A shelter divine, my heart's gentle plea.

As seasons change, I stand still,
In the well of wisdom, I find my will.
In shadows and light, the journey unfolds,
With courage embraced, my story is told.

Oh, sacred well, my endless guide,
In your depths, my fears subside.
With gratitude flowing like a stream,
I honor the wisdom, a sacred dream.

Unfolding the Path of Grace

Step by step, the path is laid,
In every choice, a promise made.
With open heart, I walk this road,
In trust and love, my spirit's abode.

The hills may rise, the valleys may fall,
Yet grace surrounds me, embracing all.
In trials faced, I find my way,
With faith as my light, come what may.

In the dance of life, I learn to sway,
With each new dawn, a brand new day.
The lessons taught in love's embrace,
Guide me gently, through time and space.

With every heartbeat, the journey unfolds,
Revealing the treasures that love beholds.
In moments of doubt, I reach for the sky,
Knowing I'm cherished, I need not ask why.

So here I stand, with arms open wide,
Embracing the grace that does abide.
In the unfolding path, my spirit takes flight,
Guided by love, I step into light.

Sacred Steps on My Journey

With faith as my guide, I move ahead,
Each step a blessing, where angels tread.
The path is holy, shining bright,
In shadows deep, I seek the light.

In every trial, a lesson found,
The whispers of grace, a soft sound.
Through valleys low and mountains high,
I walk in courage, beneath the sky.

The spirit leads where love will flow,
In sacred moments, I come to know.
My heart's embrace, divine and true,
In every rhythm, I feel anew.

With each encounter, I find my place,
In the tapestry of time and space.
The threads of mercy, woven tight,
In sacred steps, I find my light.

As dawn awakens with gentle grace,
I walk this journey, love's embrace.
In sacred steps, my soul takes flight,
Forever seeking, through day and night.

Theology of the Inner Self

In silence I ponder, within my soul,
The whispers of wisdom that make me whole.
A mirror reflects what lies deep inside,
In the quiet of prayer, my heart's confide.

The spirit dances, a mystical art,
With each breath taken, I open my heart.
In struggles and joys, the truth I find,
The theology woven, in body and mind.

The shadows and light, they blend as one,
In the depths of silence, I hear the sun.
This inner journey, a sacred quest,
In faith and reflection, I find my rest.

To understand self, is to know the divine,
In connection with all, the sacred design.
The echo of love, in every tear,
In the theology of self, all becomes clear.

Awakening spirits, with love we rise,
In the dance of existence, beneath vast skies.
With humble hearts, we seek to embrace,
The sacred within, our eternal grace.

The Table of Transformation

At the table of life, we gather near,
With open hearts, we cast out fear.
Blessings unfold with each shared meal,
In unity's bond, our souls reveal.

With love as the bread, we nourish the soul,
In acts of kindness, we come whole.
The wine of compassion, poured out anew,
In the table's light, we see what's true.

Each story shared, a thread interwound,
In the tapestry of grace, we are found.
Together we rise, in faith we stand,
In the warmth of the table, we join hand in hand.

Transformation flows, like rivers wide,
In the feast of love, we cannot hide.
Freedom unfolds in every embrace,
At the table of life, we find our place.

Let us gather often, in joy we share,
The love that we find in the hearts laid bare.
At the table of transformation, we grow,
In the sacred communion, our spirits glow.

A Soul's Exodus to Freedom

From chains of doubt, my spirit ascends,
In the exodus, where the journey bends.
With wings of hope, I soar above,
In search of the light, the essence of love.

The winds of change, they beckon me near,
In the whispers of faith, I lose my fear.
Each step I take, liberation sings,
In the heart's quiet, the freedom it brings.

Through valleys of struggle, I find my way,
With courage ignited, I greet each day.
A rising dawn, upon the hill,
In the dance of freedom, my spirit will thrill.

A journey inward, where truth resides,
In sacred stillness, my heart abides.
With every heartbeat, I shed the past,
In a soul's exodus, the die is cast.

And in this journey, I discover grace,
In the light of the divine, I find my place.
A soul's exodus, forever it yearns,
In freedom's embrace, my spirit returns.

Milton Keynes UK
Ingram Content Group UK Ltd.
UKHW020042271124
451585UK00012B/996